Funny, Wise, and
Inspirational Quotes
For Your Birthday

The
Birthday
Book

TheQuoteWell

www.TheQuoteWell.com

Words are powerful! TheQuoteWell is committed to sharing inspiration and wisdom through the power of the written word. Visit our webpage for:

- **Free quote collections**
- **Free tweetable images of inspiration**
- **Articles about Love, Life, Leadership, and more!**

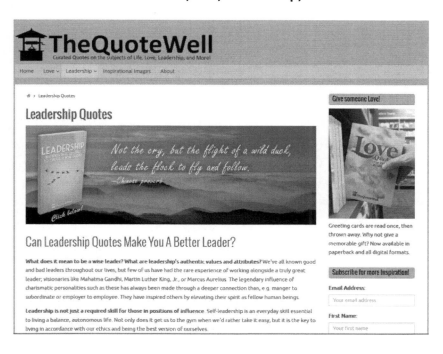

To: Michelle

From: Mom   xoxoxoxoxoxo

"Happy 50th Birthday"

This book is dedicated to you, on your birthday!

Table of Contents

Foreword

This book is the result of many hours of research. Thousands of quotes were evaluated based on their relevance to the title, their ability to inspire, and for the accuracy of their citations. Unfortunately, curating quotes is an imprecise science. Great words are often borrowed. In some cases, multiple attributions can be found. In other cases, no attribution can be given. There are also many quotes that reflect similar sentiments worded differently. In the end, it is the burden of the editor to determine which quotes are used and who receives credit. Any and all content decisions made in editing these quotes have been in service of the deeper purpose of this book; to provide humor, wisdom, and perspective to the reader.

-Darren Weaver, Contributing Editor

appy Birthday!

As a child, few days were more special than your birthday. After all, birthdays are a locally-observed holiday that celebrates your life; complete with presents, a cake, and a song just about you!

Later in life, the meaning of your birthday usually changes. Along with parties and presents come reflection, self-analysis, and perspective. And of course, what birthday would be complete without some good-natured jokes from friends about getting old?

The quotes contained in this volume have been chosen for their ability to cast both levity and illumination across your path of life and aging. To describe them as "birthday quotes" would be misleading; they are not about cake and ice cream. Instead, they explore timeless themes of wisdom, graceful aging, and life's beauty.

Some of the greatest thinkers from the past to the present are represented here, providing many lifetimes of experience that can serve as both guide and road map. And yes, there is some humor as well.

This book has been curated to explore several subjects related to birthdays, and answer some profound questions:

1) Humor about life and aging.
2) How do we define youth and old age?
3) What can we expect from each of life's stages?
4) How can we make the most of life?
5) Quotes that inspire.

Aging can be a noble and graceful process, each chapter of life filled with its own unique pleasures, gratification, and advantages. This book was given in celebration of *your* life. May it offer you both wit and wisdom.

Chapter 1
Funny Quotes About Birthdays and Growing Older

Age is just a number. Mine is unlisted. —Author unknown

It takes about ten years to get used to how old you are. —Raymond A. Michel

Wisdom doesn't necessarily come with age. Sometimes age just shows up all by itself. —Tom Wilson

Middle age is when your age starts to show around your middle.
—Bob Hope

First you forget names, then you forget faces, then you forget to zip up your fly, and then you forget to unzip your fly.
—Branch Rickey

The lovely thing about being forty is that you can appreciate twenty-five-year-old men. —Colleen McCullough

Youth is when you are allowed to stay up late on New Year's Eve. Middle age is when you are forced to. —Bill Vaughn

Life is a moderately good play with a badly written third act. —Truman Capote

Years ago we discovered the exact point, the dead center of middle age. It occurs when you are too young to take up golf and too old to rush to the net. —Franklin Adams

Old age isn't so bad when you consider the alternative.
—Maurice Chevalier

When I was a boy of fourteen, my father was so ignorant I could hardly stand to have the old man around. But when I got to be twenty-one, I was astonished at how much he had learned in seven years. —Mark Twain

Nature gives you the face you have at twenty, but it's up to you to merit the face you have at fifty. —Coco Chanel

The Best way to remember your wife's birthday is to forget it once. —H. V. Prochnow

The first half of life consists of the capacity to enjoy without the chance; the last half consists of the chance without the capacity. —Mark Twain

Middle age is when a narrow waist and a broad mind begin to change places. —Author unknown

The older I grow the more I distrust the familiar doctrine that age brings wisdom. —H.L. Mencken

Middle age is when you choose your cereal for the fiber, not the toy. —Author unknown

You know you're getting old when you get that one candle on the cake. It's like, 'See if you can blow this out.'
—Jerry Seinfeld

You know you're getting old when the candles cost more than the cake. —Bob Hope

Old age ain't no place for sissies. —Bette Davis

Middle age is when work is a lot less fun and fun is a lot more work. —Author unknown

Age does not diminish the extreme disappointment of having a scoop of ice cream fall from the cone. —Jim Fiebig

I complain that the years fly past, but then I look in a mirror and see that very few of them actually got past.
—Robert Brault

Time may be a great healer, but it's a lousy beautician.
—Author unknown

Middle age is when your classmates are so gray and wrinkled and bald they don't recognize you. —Bennett Cerf

Middle age is the awkward period when Father Time starts catching up with Mother Nature. —Harold Coffin

The secret to eternal youth is arrested development. —Alice Roosevelt Longworth

Middle age is when a guy keeps turning off lights for economical rather than romantic reasons. —Eli Cass

The best years of a woman's life: the ten years between thirty-nine and forty. —Author unknown

In youth, the days are short and the years are long. In old age, the years are short and the days long. —Nikita Ivanovich Panin

I was brought up to respect my elders, so now I don't have to respect anybody. —George Burns (at 100 years old)

Old age is like a plane flying through a storm. Once you are aboard, there is nothing you can do about it. —Golda Meir

Growing old is like being increasingly penalized for a crime you have not committed. —Anthony Powell

I'm at an age when my back goes out more than I do.
—Phyllis Diller

Inside every older person is a younger person wondering what the hell happened. —Multiple attributions

The first sign of maturity is the discovery that the volume knob also turns to the left. —Jerry M. Wright

When I was younger, I could remember anything, whether it had happened or not. But my faculties are decaying now and soon I shall be so I cannot remember any but the things that never happened. —Mark Twain

They say that age is all in your mind. The trick is keeping it from creeping down into your body. —Author unknown

Middle age is when you've met so many people that every new person you meet reminds you of someone else. —Ogden Nash

They tell you that you'll lose your mind when you grow older.
What they don't tell you is that you won't miss it very much.
—Malcolm Cowley

Youth would be an ideal state if it came a little later in life.
—Herbert Asquith

You're not forty, you're eighteen with twenty-two years
experience.
—Author unknown

One should never trust a woman who tells her real age. A woman who would tell one that would tell anything.
—Oscar Wilde

Time and Tide wait for no man, but time always stands still for a woman of thirty. —Robert Frost

Age is strictly a case of mind over matter. If you don't mind, it doesn't matter. —Jack Benny

A diplomat is a man who always remembers a woman's birthday but never remembers her age. —Robert Frost

Few women admit their age. Few men act theirs.
—Author unknown

You can live to be a hundred if you give up all the things that make you want to live to be a hundred. —Woody Allen

The brain forgets much, but the lower back remembers everything. —Robert Brault

Just remember, once you're over the hill, you begin to pick up speed. —Charles Schulz

When our vices desert us, we flatter ourselves that we are deserting our vices. —Francois Duc de La Rochefoucauld

We are young only once, after that we need some other excuse.
—Author unknown

I advise you to go on living solely to enrage those who are paying your annuities. It is the only pleasure I have left.
—Voltaire

Thirty-five is when you finally get your head together and your body starts falling apart. —Caryn Leschen

You know you've reached middle age when a doctor, not a policeman, tells you to slow down, all you exercise are your prerogatives, and it takes you longer to rest than to get tired. —Author unknown

Everything slows down with age, except the time it takes cake and ice cream to reach your hips. —John Wagner

You're never too old. Unfortunately, you're always too young to know it. —Robert Brault

I don't know how you feel about old age, but in my case I didn't even see it coming. It hit me from the rear.
—Phyllis Diller

Like many women my age, I am twenty-eight years old.
—Mary Schmich

Marriage is the alliance of two people, one of whom never remembers birthdays and the other never forgets them.
—Ogden Nash

Before thirty, men seek disease; after thirty, diseases seek men. —Chinese proverb

Wrinkled was not one of the things I wanted to be when I grew up. —Author unknown

Don't let aging get you down. It's too hard to get back up. —John Wagner

The first forty years of life give us the text. The next thirty supply the commentary on it. —Arthur Schopenhauer

I am now old enough to no longer have a fear of dying young. —Bruce Ades

To get back my youth I would do anything in the world, except take exercise, get up early, or be respectable. —Oscar Wilde

The elderly don't drive that badly. They're just the only ones with time to do the speed limit. —Jason Love

Middle age: the time when you'll do anything to feel better, except give up what is hurting you. —Robert Quillen

When the problem is not so much resisting temptation as finding it, you may just be getting older. —Author unknown

I am getting old and the sign of old age is that I begin to philosophize and ponder over problems which should not be my concern at all. —Jawaharlal Nehru

The best thing about getting old is that all those things you couldn't have when you were young, you no longer want. —L.S. McCandless

Middle age is having a choice between two temptations and choosing the one that'll get you home earlier. —Dan Bennett

Old people are fond of giving good advice. It consoles them for no longer being capable of setting a bad example.
—Francois De La Rochefoucauld

What most persons consider as virtue, after the age of forty is simply a loss of energy. —Voltaire

Age is like the newest version of a software; it has a bunch of great new features but you lost all the cool features the original version had. —Carrie Latet

When men grow virtuous in their old age, they only make a sacrifice to God of the devil's leavings. —Jonathan Swift

We are only young once. That is all society can stand.
—Bob Bowen

Regrets are the natural property of grey hairs. —Charles Dickens

Chapter 2

Perspectives on The Seasons of Life

At nineteen, everything is possible and tomorrow looks friendly.
—Jim Bishop

You make me chuckle when you say that you are no longer young, that you have turned twenty-four. A man is or may be young to after sixty, and not old before eighty.
—Oliver Wendell Holmes, Jr.

Live as long as you may; the first twenty years are the longest half of your life. —Robert Southey

I'm never so sure as I was in my mid-twenties. —Meryl Streep

When you turn thirty, a whole new thing happens; you see yourself acting like your parents.
—Blair Sabol

Forty is the old age of youth; fifty is the youth of old age.
—French proverb

From forty to fifty a man must move upward, or the natural falling off in the vigor of life will carry him rapidly downward. —Oliver Wendell Holmes, Jr.

Middle age is youth without its levity, and age without decay. —Daniel Defoe

A man who views the world the same at fifty as he did at twenty has wasted thirty years of his life. —Muhammad Ali

The heyday of a woman's life is the shady side of fifty.
—Elizabeth Staton

The years between fifty and seventy are the hardest. You are always being asked to do things, and yet you are not decrepit enough to turn them down. —T. S. Eliot

Once I was looking through the kitchen window at dusk and I saw an old woman looking in. Suddenly the light changed and I realized that the old woman was myself. You see, it all happens on the outside. Inside one doesn't change.
—Molly Keane

The great secret that all old people share is that you really haven't changed in seventy or eighty years. Your body changes, but you don't change at all. And that, of course, causes great confusion. —Doris Lessing

A man over ninety is a great comfort to all his elderly neighbors. He is a picket-guard at the extreme outpost, and the young folks of sixty and seventy feel that the enemy must get by him before he can come near their camp.
—Oliver Wendell Holmes

Where did the time go? Yesterday I was a girl, and today I suddenly find myself in the autumn of my years, with the cold winds of winter breathing down my neck.
—Peggy Toney Horton

At twenty years of age, the will reigns; at thirty, the wit; and at forty, the judgment. —Benjamin Franklin

It is in the thirties that we want friends. In the forties we know they won't save us any more than love did.
—F. Scott Fitzgerald

The old believe everything, the middle-aged suspect everything, the young know everything. —Oscar Wilde

At age twenty, we worry about what others think of us. At age forty, we don't care what they think of us. At age sixty, we discover they haven't been thinking of us at all. —Ann Landers

In youth, we learn. In age, we understand.
—Marie von Ebner-Eschenbach

Youth disserves, middle age conserves, old age preserves.
—Martin H. Fischer

Youth is a blunder, manhood; a struggle, old age; a regret.
—Benjamin Disraeli

In childhood, we yearn to be grown-ups. In old age, we yearn to
be kids. It just seems that all would be wonderful if we didn't
have to celebrate our birthdays in chronological order.
—Robert Brault

A person is always startled when he hears himself seriously
called an old man for the first time. —Oliver W. Holmes, Sr.

Old age: a great sense of calm and freedom. When the passions have relaxed their hold, you may have escaped, not from one master but from many. —Plato

The tragedy of old age is not that one is old, but that one is young. —Oscar Wilde

Old age is the most unexpected of all the things that happen to a man. —Leon Trotsky

As we grow older, our capacity for enjoyment shrinks, but not our appetite for it. —Mignon McLaughlin

The sun shines different ways in summer and winter. We shine different ways in the seasons of our lives. —Terri Guillemets

There are years that ask questions and years that answer. —Zora Neale Hurston

Each ten years of a man's life has its own fortunes, its own hopes, its own desires. —Johann von Goethe

You'll find as you grow older that you weren't born such a great while ago after all. The time shortens up.
—William Dean Howells

Thirty, thirty-five, forty, all had come to visit her like admonitory relatives, and all had slipped away without a trace, without a sound, and now, once again, she was waiting. —Evan S. Connell

What does every birthday end with? 'Y!' All the world's a stage, and all the men and women, merely players. They have their exits and entrances, and one man in his time plays many parts. —William Shakespeare

We thought we were running away from the grown-ups, and now we're the grown-ups. —Margaret Atwood

The day which we fear as our last is but the birthday of eternity. —Author unknown

Chapter 3

What is Youth? What is Old Age?

How old would you be if you didn't know how old you are?
—Satchel Paige

We are always the same age inside. —Gertrude Stein

There is a fountain of youth: it is your mind, your talents, the creativity you bring to your life and the lives of the people you love. When you learn to tap this source, you will have truly defeated age. —Sofia Loren

Nobody grows old merely by living a number of years. We grow old by deserting our ideals. Years may wrinkle the skin, but to give up enthusiasm wrinkles the soul. —Samuel Ullman

A man is not old as long as he is seeking something.
—Jean Rostand

It is not true that people stop pursuing dreams because they grow old, they grow old because they stop pursuing dreams.
—Gabriel Garcia Marquez

The aging process has you firmly in its grasp if you never get the urge to throw a snowball. —Doug Larson

Youth has no age. —Pablo Picasso

You can't help getting older, but you don't have to get old. —George Burns

You grow up the day you have your first real laugh at yourself.
—Ethel Barrymore

Aging is not lost youth, but a new stage of opportunity and strength. —Betty Friedan

Maturity has more to do with what types of experiences you've had, and what you've learned from them, and less to do with how many birthdays you've celebrated. —Author unknown

To keep the heart unwrinkled, to be hopeful, kindly, cheerful, reverent, that is to triumph over old age. —Thomas B. Aldrich

You are as young as your faith, as old as your doubt, as young as your self-confidence, as old as your fear, as young as your hope, as old as your despair. —Paul H. Dunn

One of the signs of passing youth is the birth of a sense of fellowship with other human beings as we take our place among them. —Virginia Woolf

There are people whose watch stops at a certain hour and who remain permanently at that age.
—Charles Augustin Sainte-Beuve

There is no old age. There is, as there always was, just you.
—Carol Grace

There is always some specific moment when we realize our youth is gone, but years after, we know it was much later.
—Mignon McLaughlin

It's not about turning older as the time passes, but growing more matured with all the newness of the growth.
—Mystique Madanmohan

We don't stop playing because we grow old; we grow old because we stop playing. —George Bernard Shaw

We must always change, renew, rejuvenate ourselves, otherwise we harden. —Johann Wolfgang Von Goethe

When our memories outweigh our dreams, we have grown old.
—Bill Clinton

Youth is happy because it has the ability to see beauty. Anyone who keeps the ability to see beauty never grows old.
—Franz Kafka

Everyone is the age of their heart. —Guatemalan proverb

To me, old age is 15 years older than I am. —Bernard M. Baruch

We grow gray in our spirit long before we grow gray in our hair.
—Charles Lamb

Old age puts more wrinkles in our minds than on our faces.
—Michel de Montaigne

Age is opportunity no less than youth itself. —Henry Wadsworth

A man is not old until regrets take the place of dreams.
—John Barrymore

I don't believe one grows older. I think that what happens early
on in life is that at a certain age one stands still and stagnates.
—T.S. Eliot

The deepest definition of youth is life as yet untouched by tragedy. —Alfred North Whitehead

Count your life by smiles, not tears. Count your age by friends, not years. —Author unknown

Life is not measured by the breaths we take, but by the moments that take our breath away. —Hilary Cooper

Chapter 4
Living Life to the Fullest

God gave us the gift of life. It is up to us to give ourselves the gift of living well. —Voltaire

Don't just count your years; make your years count.
—Ernest Meyers

Live as if you were to die tomorrow. Learn as if you were to live forever. —Mahatma Gandhi

The golden age is before us, not behind us.
—William Shakespeare

You are never too old to set another goal or to dream a new dream. —Les Brown

It is not how old you are, but how you are old.
—Marie Dressler

May you live all the days of your life. —Jonathan Swift

With mirth and laughter let old wrinkles come.
—William Shakespeare

Wrinkles should merely indicate where the smiles have been.
—Mark Twain

A birthday is a time to reflect on the year gone by, but to also set your goals for the upcoming year. —Catherine Pulsifer

Life is too short to be small. —Benjamin Disraeli

Live and work but do not forget to play, to have fun in life and really enjoy it. —Eileen Caddy

Live as you will have wished to have lived when you are dying.
—Christian Furchtegott Gellert

It is better to wear out than to rust out.
—Bishop Richard Cumberland

Live daringly, boldly, fearlessly. Taste the relish to be found in competition, in having put forth the best within you.
—Henry J. Kaiser

Live not one's life as though one had a thousand years, but live each day as the last. —Marcus Aurelius

Live out of your imagination instead of out of your memory.
—Les Brown

Many people realize their hearts' desires late in life. Continue learning. Never stop striving. Keep your curiosity sharp, and you will never become too old to appreciate life.
—Author unknown

Pleas'd to look forward, pleas'd to look behind, and count each birthday with a grateful mind. —Alexander Pope

Man's main task in life is to give birth to himself, to become what he potentially is. —Erich Fromm

He who is of a calm and happy nature will hardly feel the pressure of age. But to him who is of an opposite disposition, youth and age are equally a burden. —Plato

Be on the alert to recognize your prime at whatever time of your life it may occur. —Muriel Spark

There is no pleasure worth forgoing just for an extra three years in the geriatric ward. —John Mortimer

To be seventy years young is sometimes far more cheerful and hopeful than to be forty years old. —Oliver Wendell Holmes

It is possible at any age to discover a lifelong desire you never knew you had. —Robert Brault

It's hard to feel middle-aged, because how can you tell how long you are going to live? —Mignon McLaughlin

Growing old is a bad habit which a busy man has no time to form. —Andre Maurois

You're only as young as the last time you changed your mind.
—Timothy Leary

The idea is to die young as late as possible. —Ashley Montagu

Today, be aware of how you are spending your 1,440 beautiful moments, and spend them wisely. —Author unknown

Use your health, even to the point of wearing it out. That is what it is for. Spend all you have before you die. Do not outlive yourself. —Bernard Shaw

View life as a continuous learning experience. —Denis Waitley

Remember this: very little is needed to make a happy life. —Marcus Aurelius

Remember, if you ever need a helping hand, you'll find one at the end of your arm. As you grow older you will discover that you have two hands; one for helping yourself, the other for helping others. —Audrey Hepburn

Your past is not your potential. In any hour you can choose to liberate the future. —Marilyn Ferguson

Live for something rather than die for nothing.
—George Patton

The key to successful aging is to pay as little attention to it as possible. —Judith Regan

To know how to grow old is the masterwork of wisdom, and one of the most difficult chapters in the great art of living. —Henri Frederic Amiel

Those who love deeply never grow old. They may die of old age, but they die young. —A. W. Pinero

The proper function of man is to live, not to exist. I shall not waste my days in trying to prolong them. I shall use my time.
—Jack London

The quality, not the longevity, of one's life is what is important.
—Martin Luther King, Jr.

The secret to a rich life is to have more beginnings than endings.
—Dave Weinbaum

When it's all over, it's not who you were. It's whether you made a difference. —Bob Dole

Never use the passing years as an excuse for old age.
—Robert Brault

When you were born, you cried and the world rejoiced. Live your life so that when you die, the world cries and you rejoice.
—Cherokee Expression

Take care of your body. It's the only place you have to live. —Jim Rohn

The best things in life aren't things. —Art Buchwald

The life given us by nature is short, but the memory of a life well spent is eternal. —Cicero

Let us endeavor to live so that when we come to die, even the undertaker will be sorry. —Mark Twain

It is only when we truly know and understand that we have a limited time on earth, and that we have no way of knowing when our time is up, that we will begin to live each day to the fullest, as if it were the only one we had.
—Elizabeth Kubler-Ross

I am old enough to see how little I have done in so much time, and how much I have to do in so little. —Sheila Kaye-Smith

Chapter 5

Inspirational Quotes About Living

You bring magic into the world my friend, and with your magic
this world becomes a better place to live in.
—Author unknown

Your life is a gift from the Creator. Your gift back to the Creator
is what you do with your life. —Billy Mills

One today is worth two tomorrows. —Benjamin Franklin

When grace is joined with wrinkles, it is adorable. There is an unspeakable dawn in happy old age. —Victor Hugo

There is nothing permanent except change. —Heraclitus

I look back on the time I've wasted, and I'm just glad I wasted it while I still had the chance. —Robert Brault

It is through the idealism of youth that man catches sight of truth, and in that idealism he possesses a wealth which he must never exchange for anything else. —Albert Schweitzer

The advantage of being eighty years old is that one has many people to love. —Jean Renoir

It is lovely, when I forget all birthdays, including my own, to find that somebody remembers me. —Ellen Glasgow

The best birthdays of all are those that haven't arrived yet.
—Author unknown

Your birthday is a special time to celebrate the gift of 'you' to
the world. —Author unknown

Today you are you! That is truer than true! There is no one alive
who is you-er than you! —Dr. Seuss

We have to be able to grow up. Our wrinkles are our medals of the passage of life. They are what we have been through and who we want to be. —Lauren Hutton

And in the end, it's not the years in your life that count. It's the life in your years. —Abraham Lincoln

We turn not older with years, but newer every day.
—Emily Dickinson

Beautiful young people are accidents of nature, but beautiful old people are works of art. —Eleanor Roosevelt

Our birthdays are feathers in the broad wing of time. —Jean Paul Richter

As you grow older, may you grow richer in all of the most important things in life. —Author unknown

To me, fair friend, you never can be old. For as you were when first your eye I eyed. Such seems your beauty still.
—William Shakespeare

May happiness and sunshine fill your day, not only on your birthday but the whole year through. —Author unknown

Grow old along with me! The best is yet to be; the last of life, for which the first was made. —Robert Browning

Because time itself is like a spiral, something special happens on your birthday each year: the same energy that God invested in you at birth is present once again.
—Menachem Mendel Schneerson

The other day a man asked me what I thought was the best time of life. "Why," I answered without a thought, "now."
—David Grayson

The years teach much which the days never knew.
—Ralph Waldo Emerson

Do not regret growing older. It is a privilege denied to many.
—Author unknown

A man's age is something impressive. It sums up his life;
maturity reached slowly and against many obstacles, illnesses
cured, griefs and despairs overcome, and unconscious risks
taken, maturity formed through so many desires, hopes,
regrets, forgotten things, loves. A man's age represents a fine
cargo of experiences and memories.
—Antoine de Saint-Exupéry

Beautiful is old age; beautiful as the slow-dropping mellow
autumn of a rich glorious summer. In the old man, Nature has
fulfilled her work. She loads him with blessings, she fills him
with the fruits of a well-spent life, and, surrounded by his
children and his children's children, she rocks him softly away to
a grave, to which he is followed with blessings. God forbid we
should not call it beautiful. —J.A. Froude

Sow a thought, and you reap an act. Sow an act, and you reap a habit. Sow a habit, and you reap a character. Sow a character, and you reap a destiny. —Charles Reader

The bad news is time flies. The good news is you're the pilot. —Michael Althsuler

The butterfly counts not months but moments, and has time enough. —Rabindranath Tagore

The length of your education is less important than its breadth, and the length of your life is less important than its depth.
—Marilyn vos Savant

Mere longevity is a good thing for those who watch life from the sidelines. For those who play the game, an hour may be a year, a single day's work, an achievement for eternity.
—Gabriel Heatter

We have no choice of what color we're born or who our parents are or whether we're rich or poor. What we do have is some choice over what we make of our lives once we're here.
—Mildred Taylor

Birth and Death are the two noblest expressions of bravery.
—Kahlil Gibran

As we grow old, the beauty steals inward.
—Ralph Waldo Emerson

When you were born: the only day in your life, your mother
smiled when you cried. —A.P.J. Abdul Kalam

The more sand that has escaped from the hourglass of our life, the clearer we should see through it. —Jean-Paul Sartre

Every day is a birthday; every moment of it is new to us. We are born again, renewed for fresh work and endeavor.
—Isaac Watts

You were born, and with you endless possibilities, very few ever to be realized. It's okay. Life was never about what you could do, but what you would do. —Richelle E. Goodrich

If you enjoyed this book and think others might also, PLEASE leave a five star review on Amazon!

Acknowledgements

This book would not have been possible without the efforts of a hardworking team of researchers. Their discriminating sensibilities have made this a significant collection of inspiration. A special thanks also goes to TheQuoteWell, who saw the value in bringing a book like this into the world. Let inspiration be the next idea virus!

About TheQuoteWell

Words are powerful! And no words are more powerful than inspirational quotes. TheQuoteWell is passionate about spreading hope, joy, wisdom, and humor through the power of the written word. Follow us on Twitter, Facebook, YouTube, and Google+ for access to FREE wisdom daily.

TheQuoteWell books are curated collections. Each book is the result of careful selection for only the best quotes from past through present on the subjects of Love, Life, Leadership, and more! The result is a chorus of profound wisdom emanating from a fascinating diversity of speakers. If you enjoyed this volume, visit our website for other titles.

Available in paperback and all digital formats.

★★★★★ **On Amazon**

"...I can literally open the book and find genius on any page."

TheQuoteWell.com

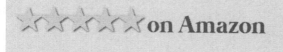on Amazon

"I enjoyed reading them to my wife."

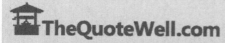

TheQuoteWell.com

 on Amazon

"...an invaluable addition to the collection of anyone who seeks to improve their life and the lives of those closest to them."

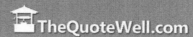TheQuoteWell.com

Made in the USA
Columbia, SC
10 November 2022

70866482R00065